MW01633010
TO:
FROM:

90 DAY DEVOTIONAL

Autumn

A Season of Thanksgiving

BroadStreet
PUBLISHING

BroadStreet Publishing Group LLC
Savage, Minnesota, USA
Broadstreetpublishing.com

Autumn: A Season of Thanksgiving

978-1-4245-5579-6

Devotional entries compiled by Michelle Winger.

Design by Chris Garborg | garborgdesign.com
Edited by Michelle Winger | literallyprecise.com

Printed in China.

18 19 20 21 22 23 24 7 6 5 4 3 2 1

You have enlarged the nation

and increased their joy;

they rejoice before you

as people rejoice

at the harvest.

Isaiah 9:3 NIV

Introduction

Autumn. It's a season of beauty. A season of reflection and gratitude. A season of sweaters and jeans, and watching flames dance on logs under a cool starry sky.

We spend time counting our blessings, jumping in leaves, and bundling up in blankets. We adapt to new schedules, consider our priorities, and make plans for the future.

This 90-day devotional will encourage you to spend some time with God, being refreshed in his presence. Experience his love, life, and goodness during this season of thanksgiving.

Leaves that Never Wither

They are like trees planted along a riverbank,
with roots that reach deep into the water.
Such trees are not bothered by the heat
or worried by long months of drought.
Their leaves stay green,
and they never stop producing fruit.

JEREMIAH 17:8 NLT

If you live in a cooler climate, then you've probably experienced the gorgeous season that is fall. Each year, the leaves slowly turn to shades of golden yellow, orange, and red. It's a thing of beauty, but eventually, the leaves wither and die, then fall to the ground.

All too often, the same can happen with our relationship with the Lord. We get that initial fire for him; we burn brightly with it, but lose our way and fall away from him. If we keep our trust in him, he tells us that our spiritual leaves will never wither. He wants our lives to be like trees that continually bear fruit.

Do your days resemble an evergreen, or do you feel like you have begun to wither? Replenish your soul by spending time in the Lord's presence. Plant your roots deeply in him, and let him water your mind, body, and spirit.

Are you bearing good fruit in your spiritual walk, or have you begun to fall away?

God, I want to burn forever bright for you. Help me to stand up to the heat and the wind if that's what faces me today. Give me the assurance that I won't fall.

Renewal

Teach me your way, Lord,
that I may rely on your faithfulness;
give me an undivided heart,
that I may fear your name.

Psalm 86:11 NIV

It's hard to find someone who doesn't love fall. The gorgeous colors; the return of scarves, sleeves, and cute boots; the peaceful silence of a home where kids have returned to their classrooms—all invite a spirit of renewal.

As the outside air begins to change and leaves begin to fall, a clean slate seems entirely possible. Think of the amazing things you could achieve in God this year. It can start today! Even when life is humming along quite nicely, the idea of a fresh beginning is irresistible. For some of us, the transition from summer to fall feels more like New Year's Day than New Year's Day does.

Spend some time dreaming with God about what this fall might bring to you, and what you might bring to it.

If God were to purify your heart, where would he begin?

God, teach me your ways. I am so hungry for you to refresh my heart and bring new things into my life. Give me a fresh perspective. As I think about this week, or the rest of the year, I ask that you show me new beginnings. Keep my heart pure so that I can clearly hear your direction.

Your Heart's Desire

Make God the utmost delight and pleasure of your life,
and he will provide for you what you desire the most.

Psalm 37:4 TPT

What did you want more than anything else in the world when you were little? Maybe having a pony or being a princess were the most delightful things you could imagine back then. What do you yearn for now? How different are your adult-sized dreams?

We've all heard that God loves to answer our prayers and to grant our desires. Should we expect him, then, to give us whatever we want? Study the verse, and notice in particular the first part. When we delight in the Lord, he gives us the desires of our heart. If we delight in financial success, washboard abs, or highly accomplished children, God makes no promises. This does not mean we are wrong for wanting these things, just that God isn't necessarily invested in making them happen for us.

When we delight ourselves in the Lord, he places desires in our heart and we realize just how well he knows us. Delight in the Lord today and see what he drops on your heart.

Take an honest look at the things you long for, dream about, and desire. What do they reveal about your relationship with God? What changes, if any, do you need to make?

God, let my heart be full of love for you before I begin to ask for provision of my desires. Let me delight in you today and always.

No Sacrifice

"I don't want your sacrifices—I want your love;
I don't want your offerings—I want you to know me."

Hosea 6:6 TLB

Imagine this: In order to prove his undying love for you, the man of your dreams just quit his job and donated all his possessions to the poor—and is now living in a tent in your front yard! Just as we would not be particularly romanced by someone proving his love by surrendering his belongings, God does not want our sacrifices.

We don't need to make a grand gesture, we just need to sit down and read his Word. He wants us to want him more than anything. He doesn't want our stuff. You may think that you haven't proven your interest in God because your days seem meaningless. You might not do anything spiritual or particularly worthy of praise.

Right now, however, you have chosen to sit down and think about the Lord. This is what he is after, your heart. Be blessed as you sit with him for a while.

When you consider the only sacrifice God wants from you is some of your undivided attention, what happens in your heart? Share this with him today.

God, I want to be with you. Thank you that I don't have to prove my love in grand gestures. You are pleased with my desire to know you. Help me to know you more even today.

He Knows

The Spirit helps us with our weakness. We do not know how to pray as we should. But the Spirit himself speaks to God for us, even begs God for us with deep feelings that words cannot explain.

Romans 8:26 NCV

There are days prayer feels like an unknown expression. We know we want something—we sense an ache or longing—but can't quite identify it. Other times, we're simply in too much pain to focus. We need, we need… but we can't get the words out.

"What do I want?" we cry. The Holy Spirit, because he lives inside us, knows us so intimately he can actually step in and pray on our behalf. He knows even when we don't.

If your day is filled with stresses of all kinds, it can be overwhelming to know where to start with the time that you have dedicated to sit down with the Lord. That's why we have the Holy Spirit.

Sometimes we don't need to use words, we just need him. Rely on him to speak on your behalf.

What is your weakness right now? Thank the Holy Spirit for knowing your heart and expressing it when you can't.

God, let your presence wash over me right now.
I need you to pray for me because I just don't have the words.
Thank you for knowing my heart.

Prepare Him Room

"He must become greater and greater,
and I must become less and less."

John 3:30 NLT

Imagine your life if all you ever did was add to your possessions. Unless we want to be featured on a certain, very popular reality television show about people with far too much stuff, bringing new things in necessitates taking old things out. We don't build a bigger closet, we go through and select which items to donate. We don't build a bigger garage, we trade the aging sedan, SUV, or minivan for a newer, better model.

So too, when we accept Christ's sacrifice and the Holy Spirit takes up residence in our hearts, we must make room. Old habits must make way for fresh, inspired new ways of being. As his presence grows inside us, the old ways diminish. When we allow Jesus to increase in our lives, things like jealousy, bitterness, and insecurity need to be bagged up and taken out so that graciousness, forgiveness, and the confidence Christ offers can move in.

Can you create room for Jesus, today? Allow your time with him to build the desire to know him more.

How much space are you allowing God right now, and how much are you holding onto for yourself?

God, help me push aside the old to create room for the new. Give me renewed joy today in knowing that you are becoming a bigger and better part of my life.

Accepting Praise

If I must boast, I will boast of the things that show my weakness.

2 Corinthians 11:30 niv

"You did an incredible job; you're so talented!" Quick, how do you respond? Going beyond thank you and actually accepting—embracing—the kind words being spoken about us is difficult for many. As little girls, we're told it's rude not to say thank you when complimented, but society, and our peers, also send an opposing message: we'd best not be perceived as boastful. So what should we do?

Accept compliments, but acknowledge that your best qualities are gifts from God. Talk freely about the ways God made you special, and how infinitely special you find him. It is freeing to learn that everything good about us is actually about Jesus. Every good gift, from beauty to a lovely singing voice to the ability to sink a three-pointer on the basketball court, is from him.

You're not full of yourself; you're full of him! Even better, every time we mess up is an opportunity to brag about his perfection. After all, we're only human. We can't do anything on our own.

Where have you messed up lately? Can you allow your weakness to be exposed to others?

God, you gave me many wonderful gifts. Help me to have humility with the things that I am good at because I know that they all come from you. Let me be a witness to your goodness.

Being Known

You know what I long for, Lord;
you hear my every sigh.

Psalm 38:9 NLT

Think of the most perfect gift you've ever received. Not the most extravagant, but the one that was just so perfectly you that you realized the giver really knew you. They heard you, that one time, when you mentioned that one thing, perhaps in passing, and because they were listening with their heart, they saw into yours. They get you.

We love to be understood, and we long to be seen. For many of us it's how we know we are loved. How much, then, must the Father love us? He who knows everything about us—who takes the time to listen to every longing and comfort every sigh—is waiting to give us his perfect gifts.

Spend some time with the one who truly understands your every thought. God knows you better than you know yourself. Take comfort in that today. You are known and you are loved. Let that thought create peace in your heart and mind.

Share your longing with God today. Let him show you his great love by revealing how intimately he knows you. Let him give you a good and perfect gift.

Father, you know exactly where my heart is and how I am feeling right now. You understand me more than anyone in this life because you created me. Help me to know that I am understood today.

Our Strength

Though the fig tree should not blossom
And there be no fruit on the vines,
Though the yield of the olive should fail
And the fields produce no food,
Though the flock should be cut off from the fold
And there be no cattle in the stalls,
Yet I will exult in the Lord,
I will rejoice in the God of my salvation.

HABAKKUK 3:17-18 NASB

The pile of bills, the noise the car is making, the layoff rumors at work, the child who stayed home sick—again. Pressures can overwhelm us especially when they accumulate. Add in the stresses we put on ourselves—*Am I good enough? Why did I say that? Other people's houses aren't this cluttered*—and you've got a potent recipe for insecurity.

When things seem impossible, and they often do, praise God that we have his promises and his power. It is not up to us to solve our problems; we need only to trust the Lord and accept his help. Do your days feel dry and unfruitful? Does everything seem to go wrong? Maybe you can't finish your tasks, or you don't react well to someone's request for you to do more work. You may have frequent arguments, or feel deflated by things somebody says to you.

Life can be hard and unfair. Praise God, anyway! He cares about your bad day, but he also cares about your heart and he is waiting to deposit some joy into a day of despair.

Where could you use a little, or a lot, of God's strength right now? Offer your worries to your Father.

God, give me assurance that I can rejoice in you even in my moments of deepest despair. Help me to see that good seasons will return once again.

True Friends

A friend loves you all the time,
and a brother helps in time of trouble.

PROVERBS 17:17 NCV

Thinking back to when you were a girl, you can probably pull up a memory of a time you thought someone was your friend only to realize you were mistaken. A revealed secret, broken promise, or perhaps a certain boy made it clear she wasn't your friend after all. Maybe you don't need to think back to your childhood. Sadly, women who are supposedly friends hurt, betray, and disappoint one another every day.

We are meant to do life together. We are meant to love one another always. Who are your friends? Those who, no matter what, have your back. Thank the Lord for them, and reach out and let them know what they mean to you. Think of the friends you want to bless. The ones who have seen—and forgiven—your worst, and who have received that same grace from you.

Whether you have one special friend, or a handful, they are treasures from God. Praise him for creating a life full of meaningful relationships.

Who can you uplift in prayer today?
Bring a friend before God in prayer.

God, thank you for my true friends. Help me to encourage and bless them today. You have given me friends that love at all times. Thank you that these friends have upheld me during my hardest moments and celebrated with me in my joys. Let me return that friendship and do the same for them.

Priorities

A shepherd should pay close attention to the faces of his flock and hold close to his heart the condition of those he cares for. A man's strength, power, and riches will one day fade away, not even nations endure forever.

PROVERBS 27:23-24 TPT

"I went online to check one thing, and the next thing I knew, two hours had passed!" How recently have you heard—or said—something similar? Our world provides endless distractions, and if we're not careful, those distractions can interfere with what we want to accomplish and who we want to be. This is why we need priorities.

Think of what you really need to get done today and make a plan to accomplish your checklist. Ask God to help you prioritize and keep focused. God's Word tells us this world is passing; today—this minute, in fact—is the only certainty. So those things we're thinking of doing someday or even next month, if they matter to us, we'd be wise to do them today.

What matters to us? Our relationships, our careers, getting to know the Father as intimately as we can? Let's be sure we give those things our full attention today and every day.

What are your priorities? Would they be obvious to someone observing a day in your life? Pray about what you discover; ask God to show you any changes you need to make.

God, just as a shepherd pays close attention to his main responsibility, let me pay close attention to the right things. Please keep me from distractions and give me self-control to focus on the right things today.

Embracing Solitude

After sending them home, he went up into the hills by himself to pray. Night fell while he was there alone.

MATTHEW 14:23 NLT

Everyone in the house is gone—for the entire weekend. How did those words make you feel? Were you considering who to call for a fun night out, or reveling in the thought of hours of uninterrupted quiet time to read, relax, and restore? Perhaps both ideas appeal to you: a little social time, and a little alone time.

Imagine Jesus slipping off, unnoticed, and going to spend time with his Father. What intimacy they must have shared; how restorative those hours of prayer must have been. Amidst the stories of ministering to crowds, feeding thousands, and untold hours spent with the twelve he chose as apostles, it's easy to miss this fact. Studying the gospels, we see a pattern emerge: he healed, then he went off to pray alone; he taught, then he climbed the mountain to pray alone; the disciples went out on the boat, and Jesus remained on the shore—alone.

How do you feel in your alone time with God? Spend a small portion of this day recharging your batteries by embracing solitude with your Creator. Whatever your feelings about solitude, ask God to give you Jesus' heart for alone time with him.

Where can you go for some alone time? Give yourself some space even if only for a few short minutes.

Jesus, thank you that you know the importance of being alone. Thank you for this moment of being alone with you before I head into another day full of others. Help this time to refresh me for the day ahead.

Silence

For God alone, O my soul, wait in silence,
for my hope is from him.

Psalm 62:5 esv

If the radio were broken in your car, would you need to fix it immediately, or would you relish the silence? Perhaps you or someone you know keeps the TV on all day for the noise.

What is it about silence that makes so many of us uncomfortable? Some of us even talk to ourselves to avoid it. Our feelings about silence often connect directly to our feelings about being alone. The radio keeps us from realizing we are alone, or from leaving us alone with our thoughts. But alone with our thoughts is exactly where God most wants to speak to us.

How can we hear him if we're partially tuned in to a song, show, or commercial? How can we listen if we never stop talking? Seek out silence today, and allow it to refresh your soul. Give your needs and your questions to God, and then wait for him to answer.

What is God filling your heart with in this moment?

God, allow me some time of silence. Right now I wait on you. Even if you don't speak, let me feel your presence so I can be restored in silence.

Fear

Fear and intimidation is a trap that holds you back.
But when you place your confidence in the Lord,
you will be seated in the high place.

PROVERBS 29:25 TPT

In the New Living Translation alone, the word *fear* appears 601 times. Primarily, it is there to remind us to fear God; in doing so, he will abate all other fears. The fear God desires from us is not one of mistrust, but one of respect and awe.

If we believe completely in God's sovereign power, if we give him all our reverence, how can we fear anything else? If he is for us, there is truly nothing to fear. Hallelujah!

Scripture says that fear holds us back. Confide in the Lord today what your greatest fears are. Let his love flood through you and sweep those fears away.

What do you fear? Lay it at the feet of God today, and place your trust in him. Know that no matter what your circumstances, your safety in him is secure.

God, I'll admit that at times I am afraid of this world and what it might bring. Please give me peace, knowing that my life is in your hands. Help me to cast aside my fears.

Just Ask Him

I call to you, God,
and you answer me.
Listen to me now,
and hear what I say.

PSALM 17:6 NCV

Ah, the first crush. "Does he like me?" we wondered aloud to our friends. "Just ask him," they answered. "You may never know if you don't ask," they counseled. A note was written, folded, and passed. We waited nervously for the reply. The whole thing was simple, but also scary.

If only answers to prayer came so simply or quickly: "Should I take this job? Marry this man? Try to have a baby now, or in a year? Check yes or no." God's Word encourages us again and again to come to him with our questions, concerns, and deepest longings. He does promise a reply, though not necessarily in the form of a check in a box.

Are there things that your heart is aching for? Do you have concerns, fears, or hopes for this week, or this year? God is waiting expectantly for your prayers, and he will answer you. It may not be today, or even for a long time, but keep asking. Keep waiting for his reply. He hears you.

What are you longing to know? Just ask God.

God, I call to you now, asking for answers. At times I am unsure if I am asking the right thing, but I know it doesn't matter because you will hear me and you will answer, even if it isn't the answer that I want.

Free to Do What?

*You, my brothers and sisters, were called to be free.
But do not use your freedom to indulge the flesh; rather,
serve one another humbly in love.*

Galatians 5:13 NIV

What would you do with a day of total freedom? All your obligations, limitations, and commitments are lifted. Do you head to a spa, a shopping mall, or your favorite coffee spot? If we're being honest, most of us considered something along these lines.

Our challenge is to see freedom a different way. Paul admonishes the Galatians to look at the liberty they have because of Christ's sacrifice not as a license to indulge but to reach out. Free of the restrictions of the Old Testament law, we needn't concern ourselves with having a clean slate, or making sure our neighbors do. We are free to meet the needs we see around us—to openly, freely love one another.

It seems odd to take our freedom and apply it to serving other people. We often feel like we deserve freedom; we expect to be able to do what we want when we want. But this isn't at all the example that Jesus gave us. He chose to serve when he could have lived for himself. Spend some time thanking God for your freedom. Think of how you can use that freedom to bless others.

If you were to apply this concept of freedom to your own life, what might you do—where might you go? Search your heart for a way you long to serve others, and begin praying about how to make it happen.

God, let me love others in freedom and without restriction. I don't want to indulge in things just because I know that I am free to do so. Let me be generous with my time and energy and use them for the sake of others.

Our Destiny

There is still a vision for the appointed time;
it speaks of the end, and does not lie.
If it seems to tarry, wait for it;
it will surely come, it will not delay.

Habakkuk 2:3 NRSV

As we listen to a talented singer, or watch a brilliant athlete, these people, so apparently effortless in their pursuits, seem born for just those things. *This is their destiny,* we think. *What is my destiny?* We may then wonder. *What was I born to do?*

You still have so much life ahead of you. Whether you are young or getting older, God has not forgotten you! He has gifted you with things that will bring him glory. Bring your talents to God, use them where you need to, and be patient for the fruitfulness. Whether or not you believe you have a specific purpose, God knows you do. And he knows just what it is, and how long—how many false starts and poor decisions—it will take you to fulfill it.

God is deeply interested in the destinies of those who call him Father, just as he is in the ultimate fate of the whole world. Talk to him about your hopes and dreams.

Are you waiting on God to fulfill—or reveal—your destiny? Take comfort in today's passage, and thank him for his perfect timing. If waiting is hard, ask for his help.

God, show me what you want me to do with my talents. Help me to recognize my gifts in the things that I do from day to day. Let me think about your glory, not my own.

No More Thirst

"Never again will they hunger;
never again will they thirst.
The sun will not beat down on them,
nor any scorching heat.
For the Lamb at the center of the throne
will be their shepherd;
he will lead them to springs of living water.
And God will wipe away every tear from their eyes."

Revelation 7:16-17 NIV

Imagine a marathon with no water stops. A sideline with no giant cooler for the team. Immediately, we picture athletes dropping from dehydration and exhaustion. It's unthinkable.

What is the most thirsty you've ever been? How long had you gone without drinking, and how wonderful did those first few sips taste when your thirst was finally quenched? Perhaps one of Jesus' most audacious promises is to take away our thirst. It's extraordinary. He will be all we need, he tells us.

Perhaps you feel spiritually dry today. Maybe you are working through something in your relationship or workplace and you don't have the creativity, time, or energy to put into it. Go back to your image of the marathon, and picture yourself running strong, completely free from thirst or pain. Ask the Holy Spirit to reveal what this might look like in your life.

What needs can Jesus meet? Thank God for the incredible promise of living water to come.

God, thank you that you will provide me with all my spiritual needs. When I am hungry, you will feed me. When I am thirsty, you will provide me with water. The heat will not burn me. I trust you to take care of me.

You Are Beautiful

You are all fair, my love,
And there is no spot in you.

SONG OF SONGS 4:7 NKJV

Stereotypes become stereotypes because of the truth in them. We think of a group of girls comparing flaws, calling themselves ugly while reassuring their friends of their beauty. We've seen it. We've heard it. We've lived it. Are you welcoming and accepting of the person you see in the mirror, or do you analyze, criticize, and judge?

As you stand before your mirror today to get ready—smile. If this is difficult for you, ask Jesus, the bridegroom, to show you what he sees. Listen to what the bridegroom says about his bride. She is altogether beautiful with no flaws. How is that even possible?

Let us believe the encouraging words of others, and silence the voice in our heads that tells us we are anything but beautiful. The voice is a lie. God's Word is truth, and he says we are beautiful.

What would it take for you to see yourself as beautiful?

God, you created me. I realize now that it pains you when I criticize myself because of the way I look. Let me look at myself with the courage that you made me beautiful and you see no flaw in me.

In Times of Doubt

God you are near me always, so close to me;
every one of your commands reveals truth.
I've known all along how true and unchanging
is every word you speak, established forever!

Psalm 119:151-152 TPT

The sun will set tonight; it will rise tomorrow. This is truth. We have no reason to doubt what we've witnessed every day of our lives. But when experience tells us otherwise, or perhaps we have no experience to go on, doubts creep in. It's going to snow tomorrow. "I doubt that," we say.

Remember, today, that God's truth is unchanging. It is sure as the sun that rose this morning and will set tonight. When someone we trust says they'll be there for us, we have faith in their words. Someone who has repeatedly let us down can make the same promise, but we remain uncertain until they've shown up and proven themselves.

Do you feel unsettled? Are you doubting? God wants to erase that doubt and he will; you only need to have faith.

Examine your prayer life. Do you trust God, or do you doubt his promises to you? Why? Share your heart openly with him, and ask him for unwavering faith.

God, just as the Psalmist wrote, you are near me always; you are so close to me. Thank you that every one of your commands reveals truth. Let me trust in your truth as I go into my day.

Victory

"Listen to me, all you men of Israel! Do not be afraid as you go out to fight your enemies today! Do not lose heart or panic or tremble before them. For the Lord your God is going with you! He will fight for you against your enemies, and he will give you victory!"

Deuteronomy 20:3-4 NLT

When we are little, an offense as small as borrowing a favorite pink marker without permission can create an enemy if only for an afternoon. We may even have sworn to hate the pretty little blonde chosen to play Cinderella.

As we grow, it takes a bit more. By the time we are women, for most of us, the concept of having an actual enemy is pretty foreign. That little girl, so incensed over the pink marker or Cinderella, is adorably amusing. We do have an enemy though, and he would like nothing more than to steal our joy and assure our defeat. His weapons? Jealousy, insecurity, and vanity, just to name a few.

Do you feel like some of your days are a battle? Some days are easier than others, but the Lord has given you what you need to defeat those things that come against you to try and discourage you. Don't panic, don't tremble, because God is with you in battle! Rejoice!

What enemy are you fighting? Ask, and then allow God to fight for you, and be assured of your victory.

God, protect me against the enemy today. Keep my mind from dwelling on jealousy or insecurity. Let me think on your goodness as my defense!

True Healing

O Lord, if you heal me, I will be truly healed;
if you save me, I will be truly saved.
My praises are for you alone!

Jeremiah 17:14 NLT

Examine your scars, and recall the wounds that gave them to you. Depending on the severity of the injury, and how long ago it occurred, running a finger along the scar may bring back vivid memories of the pain you felt. You are healed but also changed.

It may be painful, but explore your old heart wounds, the ones that never seem to entirely heal. Broken bones mend, but a limp or occasional twinge may remain. So might our fear; it can take a lifetime to fully trust our healing is complete—except for when God does the healing.

When we ask God to remove old hurts, betrayals, and disappointments from our hearts, he removes them completely. Begin today the process of releasing them to God, and claim the promise of his true healing.

What has God healed you or saved you from? Thank him!

God, I have been hurt in my life. I'm thankful that you have healed me, but sometimes remembering the hurt brings the pain back. Please remind me that I was saved from hurt and help me to dwell on your healing.

Nobody's Perfect

Whoever keeps the whole law but fails in one point has become accountable for all it.

James 2:10 esv

Let's say you have a teenage daughter, and you're leaving her home alone. You trust her, but just so there are no misunderstandings, you leave her a list of no's: no parties, no boys in the house, no announcing on social media that you're home alone. Let's say she invites her boyfriend over. Even though she followed most of your instructions, she still broke the rules. Bring on the consequences.

God's law is no different, and that is why we need Jesus. We've broken the rules; bring on the consequences. Or admit what he already knows. We aren't perfect. While we may never kill or steal or eat the wrong thing on the wrong day, we are entirely likely to covet, to take the easy way out, or to gossip.

Because of grace we get to choose: follow all the rules, or accept his forgiveness in advance. Spend some time thanking him for his incredible, undeserved gift of grace.

What do you choose: your ability to keep every command, or God's grace?

Thank you, God, for gifting me with immeasurable grace! Let me walk in freedom today.

Please Remain Seated

"Remain in me, as I also remain in you. No branch can bear fruit by itself; it must remain in the vine. Neither can you bear fruit unless you remain in me."

JOHN 15:4 NIV

When riding in a moving car, boat, or plane, we wouldn't just jump out, no matter how restless or impatient we were feeling. That would be crazy. We couldn't possibly expect to arrive at our destination as safely or as quickly—or perhaps at all. We grasp the necessity of remaining where we are if we are to get where we are going.

Why, then, are we so quick to jump ahead when it comes to God's plans for our lives?

Spend some time praying for the Spirit to reveal to you anywhere you are not abiding in Jesus, or trusting his timing. Ask him to help you trust him.

Are you impatient about what God is or isn't doing in your life? We seem to accept God's grace, but not his timing. We welcome his comfort, but not his discipline. How often do we decide without praying, or act without his prompting? And yet we expect to get where we are going—safely, quickly, easily. Remain in Jesus because this is where you are finally going to see fruit.

Are there areas of your life you are trying to direct on your own?

Jesus, I want to remain in you by staying close by your side as we walk this journey together. Help me to trust that you are bringing me with you and not leaving me alone.

Not Our Power

We have this treasure in jars of clay, to show that the surpassing power belongs to God and not to us.

2 CORINTHIANS 4:7 ESV

We've all heard a story: a 110–pound mother stops a moving car with her bare hands, or defeats a charging bear, to save her toddler. We love the image of the tiny defeating the mighty. The sheer unlikeliness of it is what makes it so compelling; love will make the impossible possible.

When we feel called to do something for God, our first instinct may be to list our shortcomings. We focus on our ability, our strength, forgetting the One who promises to equip us with all we need. We are like Esther, wondering, *What if I fail?* The fact we could easily fail is what makes it a great story.

Have you felt God prompting you to do something that seems impossible? What if all you had to do was agree to try? Maybe you dream of accomplishing something but don't believe you could. What if he gave you that dream, and he's just waiting for you to ask for his help? As you rest, reflect on those dreams. Ask for his power to accomplish them.

What are the dreams that God wants to restore to your heart?

God, I know you have called me to love you and love others.
I know that you have given me specific gifts for a specific time.
I rely on your power, not my own strength,
to do these things for you.

Trust the Light

"I am the Light of the world; he who follows Me will not walk in the darkness, but will have the Light of life."

John 8:12 nasb

Imagine yourself in total darkness, perhaps a wilderness camping trip (or a power failure at a nice hotel if that's more your speed). It's the middle of the night, and you must find your way back to camp. Turn on your flashlight. Though it only illuminates a few steps at a time, it's enough to keep moving. Each step forward lights more of the way, and eventually, you see your destination.

Jesus is our light. He shows us just what we need to see to put one foot forward at a time. Our faith walk is very much like needing a flashlight to light our step. Most of the time, we can't see where we're headed. Although just a few steps ahead is all we can make out for certain, we trust the path the light reveals.

Even though the night takes away the sun, we can be sure that it will rise again in the morning. Rest in the assurance that Jesus always lights the way. Ask him to help you ignore the unseen and trust the light.

What do you need God to illuminate for you right now?

**God, give me enough light to see the next step.
I am ready to move forward in you and so I ask for your
revelation and wisdom of where to go next.**

Living by Faith

In my distress I cried out to the Lord;
yes, I prayed to my God for help.
He led me to a place of safety;
he rescued me because he delights in me.

Psalm 18:6,19 NLT

In the previous devotion, we pictured being led by a single beam of light, allowing its illumination to direct our steps. The flashlight helped us avoid a tangle of roots, or a dangerous drop-off. Take the journey a little deeper today, and imagine the batteries giving out. Once again, you're in darkness. What now? Cry for help. Ask someone who is already there to guide you.

This again, is our faith walk. While Jesus' light never goes out, sometimes our sight does. We get so bogged down by circumstances, by sin, by our own agendas, we can't see a thing. How do we keep moving? We cry out, and then we follow the sound of God's voice. We must step more slowly now, but we can still walk. We just need to listen, and have faith in his voice.

Can you think of a time where you honestly couldn't see where you were headed? Perhaps that time is now.

Are there steps you need to take in spite of your blindness to the path? Call out to God. Let his voice guide you home.

God, I know that you are always ready to rescue me, but I also know that I need to acknowledge my distress, so I call out to you and plead with you to rescue me. Thank you for hearing my cry.

Trying to Please

*"Blessed are those who are persecuted for righteousness' sake,
For theirs is the kingdom of heaven."*

MATTHEW 5:10 NKJV

Think of a time you took a stand for your faith. Risking disapproval, you retained your purity despite pressure to join this century. You confronted friends in the midst of a gossipy discussion. You declined another invitation to an all-night party/husband-bashing session. Scary, wasn't it?

We want to be liked. God made us for community. Most women crave harmony, so expressing an unpopular or old-fashioned opinion can be daunting. But what is the alternative? Think now of the last time you didn't take a stand for your faith. How did you feel afterward?

We were never promised this life would be easy. In fact, Scripture repeatedly points to the opposite. Resisting the world is hard; without the help of the Holy Spirit, it's actually impossible. Where do you need help living to please God and not people? Ask him to help you, and know that he will. And when you fail, know that he has already forgiven you.

Who is your opposition to the faith right now?
What steps can you take to stand up for your faith?

God, thank you that this faith in you is true and real and right. I pray that I would always stand up for this faith and that you would bless me as others mock me (silently or not) for my beliefs.

Our Comforter

Praise be to the God and Father of our Lord Jesus Christ, the Father of compassion and the God of all comfort, who comforts us in all our troubles, so that we can comfort those in any trouble with the comfort we ourselves receive from God.

2 Corinthians 1:3-4 NIV

Notice the repetition in the verses above. The word comfort appears four times. This isn't because Paul was feeling uninspired; it's because he wanted to make sure we heard him. We are comforted so that we can comfort. God wants both for us.

At the end of a long, difficult day, all you want to do is crawl in bed, wrap up in your comforter, and rest. Something about a soft, fluffy blanket helps problems seem less like problems.

One of God's many names is the God of all comfort. He is our ultimate comforter, allowing us to wrap ourselves in him and be warmed, reassured, and relieved. He does this so we can pay it forward, wrapping ourselves around others in need of comfort, and showing them his love.

In what ways do you need God to comfort you now?

God, thank you for your comfort. I am confident in your love, so I ask that I would be someone who is able to comfort others today. Thank you that you give me enough love for a lifetime. Give me an opportunity to share that today.

Everything in Love

Do everything in love.

1 Corinthians 16:14 NCV

What goes through your mind as you shop for groceries? How about during your workouts? While you read, or watch TV, do your thoughts turn to love? As you do dishes, is there love in the way you rinse a glass, or as you dry a pot?

First Corinthians contains the rather extraordinary command to do everything in love. *Everything.* What would that look like? How does one pick lovingly through packages of strawberries, searching for the reddest, juiciest ones? Is there a loving way to scrub the broiler pan? Perhaps not, but we most certainly can approach our daily lives in a state of love, filled with it, thereby assuring all we do will be done in love.

We can carry the love of God through our day and impact those around us with his goodness. When you choose to set your mind on something, it becomes a habit to continue thinking about that thing. Set your mind on love and watch it spill out around you. Rather than consider how to bring more love to your activities, ask to be filled to the brim with love. From there, simply let it flow.

What people or places is God calling you to share his love with?

God, I am so grateful for your mercy and grace. I know that I am forgiven and free because of your great love. I know that everything you have done has been done because you are love. Let me have a portion of that love so I can show this love to the world.

Finding Peace

You will keep in perfect peace
all who trust in you,
all whose thoughts are fixed on you!

Isaiah 26:3 NLT

What does chaos look like in your world? Crazy work deadlines, over-scheduled activities, long to-do lists and short hours? All the above? How about peace? What does that look like?

Most of us immediately picture having gotten away, whether to the master bathroom tub or a sunny beach. It's quiet. Serene. The trouble with that image, lovely as it is, is that it's fleeting. We can't live in our bathtubs or in Fiji, so our best bet is to seek out peace right in the middle of our chaos. Guess what? We can have it. Jesus promises peace to all who put him first.

How appealing is it to imagine being unmoved by the stresses in your life? Is it easy or difficult for you to imagine claiming this promise for yourself? Ask Jesus to grant you true peace; fix your thoughts on him and watch the rest of the world fade away. When it tries to sneak back in, ask him again.

What are you burdened by today? Fix your eyes on Jesus and allow him to bring peace into that situation.

God, I fix my eyes on you because I know that is the only way that I will find peace in my crazy world today. Bring peace despite everything that will go on around me.

Source of Life

With joy you will draw water
from the wells of salvation.

Isaiah 12:3 NIV

There's a reason that the Bible refers to water hundreds of times. We have a continual thirst that needs to be satisfied. Our bodies themselves are made up of water. Crops will not grow without water, and without them we'd have no sustenance. Water is the source of all life.

Jesus referred to himself as living water, and isn't it a fantastic analogy? When we have thirst for water, we drink, and it restores our bodies. And when we have a drought in our spiritual life, we need only seek him, and he will restore our soul. We never need to desire anything else but him because he will satisfy our spiritual dryness for our entire lives. We will never thirst again.

Are your days exhausting or uplifting? Are you drinking from the cup that Jesus is offering you? Or are you searching out other things to dampen the drought in your life before you seek him? Everything needs water to survive, but God doesn't merely want survival for you. He wants to give you a supernatural quenching of the thirst in your life.

Which parts of your life need to be thriving?

God, I don't just want to survive, I want to thrive. I pray that you would reach out to me as I set aside this small part of my day to seek you. Help me to find your words that will sustain me for the day to come.

Slow to Speak

Whoever guards his mouth and tongue
Keeps his soul from troubles.

PROVERBS 21:23 NKJV

It's no secret; women love to talk. Get a bunch of women in one room, and there are times that you cannot hear yourself think over the sound of the chatter. We are often quick to cut in with a thought because our minds race constantly with all that we have to say.

Nowhere in the Bible does it say, "You really should speak before thinking. Say what you want when you want to." Instead, it tells us to be quick to listen and slow to speak (see James 1:19). That's not an easy thing for us to do especially when it seems we are built to talk.

When you get home from your day, do you have a strong desire to talk about it? There's a need for us to unload all thoughts and feelings about the good and bad of a day. Sometimes, however, we forget the importance of listening. When we are more guarded with what we say and how much we say, we become better listeners. Try to be a good listener today.

Listen for the word that God has planted in you today.
He wants to talk with you. Are you willing to listen?
Take a moment to hear what he has for you.

God, keep me out of trouble today. At times I let my mouth speak, unguarded, and I have regretted those times. Instead, help me to guard what I say so I avoid trouble.

Mixed Messages

With the tongue we praise our Lord and Father, and with it we curse human beings, who have been made in God's likeness. Out of the same mouth come praise and cursing. My brothers and sisters, this should not be.

James 3:9-12 NIV

Have you ever spent Sunday morning in a pew, proclaiming your love for God, then walked out and said to a friend, "Did you see Sally's skirt? It was so short!" Perhaps you judged as someone darted in fifteen minutes late to the service. Maybe you told yourself that you're a better person than Susie because Susie yells at her kids and you rarely yell at anybody.

If so, you're not alone. It's our natural tendency to put others down to make ourselves feel better. We hold the secret belief that if someone else looks bad, we'll look good by comparison. But the Bible tells us that we cannot praise Jesus and curse others at the same time.

Your words are a direct measure of your heart. You can't have a gracious heart and then speak something judgmental. Nor can you speak of forgiveness when your heart is bitter. The Scriptures say it is impossible. Keep careful watch over your thoughts and words today being sure to lift others up as you climb closer to God.

What words have you been using for good today?
What words are causing you to check
the heart of the matter?

God, you know my heart. If I have been saying unkind or unwise things, please deal with the matter in my heart. I can't change what comes out of my mouth if I don't seek forgiveness and mercy. Help me to be kind from the inside out.

Where Credit Is Due

*"Give praise to the Lord, proclaim his name;
make known among the nations what he has done,
and proclaim that his name is exalted.
Sing to the Lord, for he has done glorious things;
let this be known to all the world."*

ISAIAH 12:4-5 NKJV

You achieve a goal, or you get some wonderful news. The day you've been waiting for has arrived, and you're so excited about it. What is your first reaction? Do you update your status on social media to let your friends know what you've done? Do you call your mom and tell her the wonderful news?

Are you giving credit where it's due? Be sure to take some time today to thank the Lord for all that he has helped you achieve, and for all that he has given you. He wants to share in your excitement.

There's nothing wrong with sharing your excitement with others. But when doing so, be sure to first give the glory and praise to God. He has given you everything you have. Get excited about how good God has been to you. When you're just so happy that you can't help but dance for joy, be sure to give Jesus a twirl too. He wants to celebrate with you!

What wonderful things has God done for you lately?

God, when I have achieved great things, I know it is only because you have gifted me with skills, opportunities, and courage. My praise is for you first.

Seeing the Good

Then God said to Abraham, "As for Sarai your wife, you shall not call her name Sarai, but Sarah shall be her name. I will bless her, and indeed I will give you a son by her. Then I will bless her, and she shall be a mother of nations; kings of peoples will come from her." Then Abraham fell on his face and laughed, and said in his heart, "Will a child be born to a man one hundred years old? And will Sarah, who is ninety years old, bear a child?"

Genesis 17:15-17 NASB

Are you a glass-half-full person, or do you live your life looking for the next tragedy to strike? It can be tempting to dismiss the good we see in our lives because we're too busy being on the lookout for the negative.

God wants to honor those who are obedient to him, and sometimes his blessings are so good they're almost unbelievable. Even Abraham, so blessed by God that he was chosen to father a nation, laughed when God gave him good news.

God gave Abraham and Sarah a promise that seemed too good to be true. Will you listen for God's promises in your life today? Look past the pain, the hurt, the trouble in your life. Can you spot the good? Don't laugh it off! Reflect on your blessings and rejoice in them.

What good things are happening around you right now?
What good things are happening in the world?

God, I know you are a good God, but sometimes I think those amazing blessings are only for a few people. Help me to hold on to your promises with faith.

My Way

The mind governed by the flesh is death, but the mind governed by the Spirit is life and peace. The mind governed by the flesh is hostile to God; it does not submit to God's law, nor can it do so. Those who are in the realm of the flesh cannot please God.

Romans 8:6-8 NIV

Most women have a stubborn streak, and they come by it honestly. They've spent so much time caring for others that they have learned to do it incredibly well. To put it plainly, they just don't want anybody else telling them how to do something because they know they can do it better.

Because of this, it can be really difficult to let go of our own way of doing things and release our lives to God. This will only backfire on us in the long run. The Bible tells us that if we are guided by the Spirit, we will live in peace.

Do you notice subtle ways that your thought patterns are changed by allowing the Holy Spirit into your decisions? Continue to be intentional about submitting your life to what he has for you. Pray for a spirit of obedience. You may be fabulous at what you do on your own, but God has even greater things in store for you if you'll only give him a chance.

How can you submit your decisions to God?

God, help me to be governed by you today. As I make decisions, whether big or small, let me seek your thoughts and your ways so I can have life and peace.

Like You Mean It

"'If you can'?" said Jesus. "Everything is possible for one who believes." Immediately the boy's father exclaimed, "I do believe; help me overcome my unbelief!"

MARK 9:23-24 NIV

When you pray, are you doing it in a spirit of boldness, or are you praying weak prayers? It's as if we are afraid to bother God with our requests. For goodness sake, we better not pester him too much, or perhaps he won't answer them at all, right? So we speak tentatively, "Dear Lord, if it is your will, it'd be great if you could..." "Father, I know you have so much on your plate, but I'd love it if...."

Let's stop with the weak prayers. You're not a wimp; you're a warrior! God knows your heart already. Believe that he can do what you are asking. There is no need for caution with the Father who loves you so dearly. Jesus said so himself.

Do you believe that God can make things possible in your life? We know that he's not a genie, granting every wish, but he is a good Father who wants the best for you. Step out boldly in faith, beginning with your prayer life. Are you talking to God in a spirit of timidity? Ask him for help in overcoming your disbelief. Everything is possible for those who believe, so set your heart upon doing so.

What things feel impossible for you right now?
Boldly approach God to give you the possibilities.

Father God, thank you that you care about what is best for me. I pray, in faith, that you would give me breakthrough in the areas that I have been asking for your guidance, healing, and support.

Game of Opinions

I, therefore, the prisoner of the Lord, beseech you to walk worthy of the calling with which you were called, with all lowliness and gentleness, with longsuffering, bearing with one another in love, endeavoring to keep the unity of the Spirit in the bond of peace.

Ephesians 4:1-3 NKJV

As soon as you accepted Christ as your Savior, you were welcomed into a special group. As Christians, we are called to live a life set apart because our actions should reflect Christ himself. But all too often, we get caught up in a game of opinions, and we begin bickering amongst ourselves about right and wrong.

Whether the topic is what women should wear, or how we should vote, or even whether to vaccinate, people have strong opinions. And heaven forbid anyone should have an opposing one!

If you've ever read the comments section on an online article or social media posting, then you've seen how ugly it can get, and how quickly. So, what happened to peace? When did we stop showing each other our love? Remember this verse today, and be humble, gentle, and patient with one another. The world needs to see our unity.

Are you living a life that is worthy of the calling you received as a Christian? Pray for a spirit of love and peace today.

God, instead of indulging in topics of discord, help me to be disciplined to promote humility, grace, and love to my brothers and sisters in Christ. I know I don't get it right every day. Forgive me when I have engaged in thoughts or actions that have been unkind. Help love to be my highest goal as I go into each day.

Ruled with Grace

The law came to make sin worse. But when sin grew worse, God's grace increased. Sin once used death to rule us, but God gave people more of his grace so that grace could rule by making people right with him. And this brings life forever through Jesus Christ our Lord.

Romans 5:20-21 NCV

God's law was given so that people could see how sinful they were. But instead, we began to sin more and more. You'd think God would've given up on us; instead, he gave us grace in abundance. We make terrible decision after terrible decision, and still he loves us and shows his mercy.

Though we deserve to be punished for our faults, God rules with his wonderful grace. Jesus died so that we would be given the gift of eternal life in heaven. Think of all the sacrifices you make for others, and then consider what it would take to sacrifice yourself so that others could live. Talk about the gift of a lifetime!

Spend some time thanking the Lord for the great gift he has given you today. Whereas once we might have lived under the law alone, now we live in grace and mercy. Let us not forget the sacrifice God made for us.

Are there things that God is calling you do for his kingdom?
Will they require sacrifice?

Jesus, I am humbled by the sacrifice that you made for humanity—that you made for me. Help me to live a life that is working toward the same goal of restoration even if that means great sacrifice.

Weary to the Core

*The steps of the God-pursuing ones
follow firmly in the footsteps of the Lord.
And God delights in every step they take to follow him.*

PSALM 37:23-24 TPT

Have you ever been run so ragged that you just didn't know if you could take even one more step? Your calendar is a blur of scheduled activities, your days are full, your every hour is blocked off for this or that, and it's hard to find even a spare minute for yourself. Even your very bones feel weary, and you fall into your bed at night drained from it all.

Are you allowing the Lord to guide your days? Though you may be weary, he has enough energy to get you through it all. Hold out your hand to him today and walk side-by-side in his strength. He is ready to catch you when you fall. You may stumble through your busy day, but he will never let you hit the floor as you take a tumble.

God delights in you! He will direct your every step if you ask him to. He will gladly take you by the hand and guide you.

How has the Lord lifted you up today?

Walk with me today, Jesus. Let each of my steps be directed by you so that I do not grow weary. Give me enough energy for today.

Relevant Now

The word of God is living and active, sharper than any two-edged sword, piercing until it divides soul from spirit, joints from marrow; it is able to judge the thoughts and intentions of the heart.

HEBREWS 4:12 NRSV

Sometimes it feels as though the Bible isn't relevant. After all, these stories took place thousands of years ago. Old Testament people lived for hundreds of years. We can't fathom being swallowed by a fish when we try to avoid God's presence. Rainbows are beautiful, but it's hard to picture the entire earth being covered in water, so we forget that rainbows are a symbol of his covenant with us.

The Word of God is alive today and just as relevant as it was for the original readers. Love, joy, peace, patience, kindness, goodness, faithfulness, gentleness, and self-control—these attributes are waiting for you if you dive in and seek them out.

As you read the stories of the Bible, search for the truth woven throughout every word in Scripture. There is much to relate to! Deborah was an amazing leader. Ruth and Naomi show a picture of friendship and love. Mary Magdalene went through struggles and was healed. Esther was incredibly brave. The Bible is truth. It always has been and always will be. Ask God to show you the relevance specific Scriptures have for you today.

Are you giving yourself time to read God's Word?
Challenge yourself to read a bit deeper this week.

God, give me inspiration as I read your Word. Allow me to see the deeper truth and to get life from what I read. Let me take your Word out into the world today!

Hidden Blessings

"Blessed are those who mourn,
for they will be comforted."

MATTHEW 5:4 NIV

There are hidden blessings to be found in the middle of our troubles. One of them is that we are better able to care for others and show compassion when we have been there ourselves. God is the source of all comfort, and he teaches us this gift as well.

The Lord shows us mercy and gives us peace that passes understanding even in the middle of our greatest pain. Because of this, when others are troubled and struggling, we have learned the true meaning of comfort and we're able to pass it along. When we walk through difficulties, one of the beautiful things that comes from those times is the ability to draw near to God and receive his unlimited supply of comfort.

Do you know someone who is going through some sort of battle? Think back to the ways God reached out to you during your time of pain. Use that knowledge to bring comfort to your friend. Who better to learn from than God himself?

Who is the Holy Spirit leading you to show comfort to? In what ways can you comfort them?

God, thank you for the comfort that you have given me, often through the kindness of other people. Let me be a comfort to those who need it today.

Working Together

God has so composed the body, giving greater honor to the part that lacked it, that there may be no division in the body, but that the members may have the same care for one another. If one member suffers, all suffer together; if one member is honored, all rejoice together. Now you are the body of Christ and individually members of it.

1 Corinthians 12:24b-27 ESV

The Bible tells us that God knit us together in our mothers' wombs. Before we were born, our bodies were carefully selected and created by our Maker, ensuring that each part worked with the others to function on the whole. Great care was put into this process.

As Christians, we are all a part of the body of Christ. Are you in tune with others in the body who are rejoicing or hurting? Just like our physical bodies, if each part is working together with the others, then the entire body functions well and is happy. But if just one part is suffering, the entire body suffers.

Spend some time praying for some of the Christians you know who come to mind. Look for ways in which you can contribute to the harmony of the body around you.

What care are you taking to be sure that the body of Christ, your community of believers, is working together? Are you rejoicing together?

God, show me the part that you would have me play in your church. Thank you that care so much about the community of believers. Help me to care for the unity and love the body of Christ as well.

Flip the Switch

The lovers of God walk on the highway of light,
and their way shines brighter and brighter
until they bring forth the perfect day.
But the wicked walk in thick darkness,
like those who travel in a fog
and yet don't have a clue why they keep stumbling!

PROVERBS 4:18-19 TPT

Have you ever walked through your home at night, thinking that you could make it without turning a light on, only to stumble on something unexpectedly set in your path? When you cannot see where you are going, you are likely to get tripped up. On the other hand, your way is obvious when you simply turn on a light.

The Bible tells us that walking in righteousness is just like walking in the bright light of day. But choosing rebellion is like stumbling around in a deep darkness. You never know what hit you until it's already too late. Are you choosing the light? Is your path brightly lit? Or are you standing in total darkness? If so, then flip the switch.

When you walk in the light, you expose the darkness, even in the lives of others around you. Pray that you will make wise choices. Seek his wisdom for your life. He wants to shine brightly for you. Let him in, and he will gladly be your eternal light, illuminating your days.

How can you bring light in a world of darkness?

God, let your light in me be a positive influence on the life of others around me. I often see darkness in the world around me and I get discouraged. Encourage my soul as I prepare to bring your light to the world each day.

Choosing Wisdom

Happy is the man who is so anxious to be with me that he watches for me daily at my gates, or waits for me outside my home! For whoever finds me finds life and wins approval from the Lord. But the one who misses me has injured himself irreparably. Those who refuse me show that they love death.

Proverbs 8:34-36 TLB

The word wisdom is used hundreds of times in the Bible. Time and time again, we are instructed to use good judgement, to make sound decisions, to use prudence and circumspection. King Solomon made a special point to ask God to give him wisdom throughout his time as Israel's leader. Because of this, God honored and blessed him.

The interesting thing is that wisdom is often referred to in Scripture as a "she." In Proverbs, she beseeches us to find her, to choose her. She tells us that if we do, we will find favor with God.

Spend some time at wisdom's doorway today. True happiness is found there, and the Lord will honor your decision!

Are you choosing wisdom? Are you seeking her out?

God, I long for your wisdom. I cannot trust my own wisdom or even the wisdom of those around me because I know that the world can be so foolish. Give me joy as I respond to your words of truth today.

Building Your House

"Everyone who hears these words of mine and puts them into practice is like a wise man who built his house on the rock. The rain came down, the streams rose, and the winds blew and beat against that house; yet it did not fall, because it had its foundation on the rock."

MATTHEW 7:24-27 NIV

Building a house can be really fun for some and really stressful for others. There's so much to choose, and so many details to go over. Color schemes, cabinet choices, carpeting, and... the list goes on and on.

Building your spiritual house is easy. The only thing you need to worry about is choosing the right foundation. Jesus himself gives us his instructions on how to do so. Sometimes we look at other people's lives—their houses—and we are envious. They look grander, newer, cleaner.

We never know what the foundation of people's lives are. They may be facing a lot of emotional, financial, or relational difficulty. Even the grandest of homes will come crashing to the ground if it is not built on solid ground.

Are you building your spiritual house on a solid foundation? Listen for God's words, and put them into practice in your daily living.

God, I choose to listen to your words today. Let me be just like the wise man who built his house on the rock. I don't want to crumble when the storms of life come, so make me stronger and stronger as I listen more and more to you!

Finding Love

Those who say, "I love God," and hate their brothers or sisters, are liars; for those who do not love a brother or sister whom they have seen, cannot love God whom they have not seen.

1 John 4:20 NRSV

The harsh reality is that if we have hardness in our hearts toward a fellow believer, we cannot truly claim to love God. Ouch.

God told us to love our neighbors as ourselves. He calls us to be one with the body of Christ. Yet, we often find fault with our brothers and sisters in the church—to the point where we can't find love for them at all. It's not what God wants for us.

Have you been able to show someone love recently, even if you felt like they didn't deserve it? If there is someone within your community of believers whom you struggle to love, pray that the Lord will give you the supernatural power to do so. It's only through God that we can find the strength to love those we couldn't otherwise.

Who do you need to change your heart attitude about?
In what ways will you show them love?

God, I love you and I know this means that I need to love others. Forgive me for the times when I have not acted in love toward someone. Help me to love you through my love to others around me. Give me an opportunity to put this into practice today.

Lighthouses

"You are the light of the world. A town built on a hill cannot be hidden. Neither do people light a lamp and put it under a bowl. Instead they put it on its stand, and it gives light to everyone in the house."

Matthew 5:14-15 NIV

There's a good reason why lighthouses were built. For hundreds of years, they've shined brightly across harbors around the world, guiding ships safely to shore. The premise was simple; put the light up high where it can easily be seen.

Jesus is the light of the world. That light wasn't meant to be hidden away. It's meant to be put up high, where everyone can easily see it. And as his followers, we are called to shine brightly for him in such a way that others can see it for themselves. We don't hide it away; we boldly light the way to Christ.

Don't keep your light for Christ hidden away bringing it out only when it feels comfortable. Pray that you will have the boldness of faith to be a source of light for everyone with whom you come in contact. Ask the Lord to help you shine brightly so that others can step out of the darkness and join you in the light.

In what ways does the world drag you down?
How can you be a light in the darkness?

God, let me be a lighthouse to a world around me
that desperately needs to see your love and life.
Guide my actions today to reflect you.

Choose Obedience

"In that I command you today to love the Lord your God, to walk in His ways and to keep His commandments and His statutes and His judgments, that you may live and multiply, and that the Lord your God may bless you in the land where you are entering to possess it."

DEUTERONOMY 30:16 NASB

The Word of God is pretty clear. Though we often want to ignore it, or walk away for a while, if we are seeking his wisdom there is no getting around the fact that we need to choose obedience.

The Bible tells us over and over that we are to keep God's commands. If we do so, we will find blessings in our lives. If not, life looks pretty bleak. It's not always easy to choose a life of obedience. Our fleshly desires spring up constantly, getting in the way of what we are called to do.

In the long run, walking with the Lord is choosing a life filled with joy. Our earthly possessions and ambitions will only leave us feeling flat. Pray for a spirit of obedience so that God can increase his blessings in your life. Walk side by side with him today, seeking his will. Choose obedience; choose joy!

In what ways do you need to experience God's forgiveness tonight?

God, remind me of your commands today. Remind me of when I am overstepping the gracious boundaries that you have given, and remind me that you place these there to keep me safe.

New Life

The Lord is good to all,
and his mercy is over all that he has made.

Psalm 145:9 ESV

Have you ever laid in bed at night, thinking over past wrongdoings and beating yourself up over decisions you made years ago? If so, you are not alone. We can be incredibly hard on ourselves, asking for near perfection.

There is good news for us all. Once we accept Christ as our Savior, we are made new. There is no need to continue to berate ourselves for the choices of the past. He has washed away our sins and made us clean. We don't have to look at life from our former point of view because our old lives are gone and new life has begun.

Release your past to the Lord. If you struggle to get past a mistake you once made, ask him for help in forgiving yourself. You have been made new in the eyes of the Lord. There is so much freedom in this knowledge. Enjoy it today!

What are you regretting? Give it over to God and move on!

Thank you, Almighty God, for your forgiveness. Thank you that the past is forgotten by you, and that I can move forward in this new day, this new life, that you have given me.

Losing to Gain

"If you try to hang on to your life, you will lose it.
But if you give up your life for my sake, you will save it."

MATTHEW 16:25 NLT

The key to growing in your faith is simple. There must be less of us in order to have more of God. To allow more of his presence into our lives, we must give up more of ourselves. We need to place our lives before him as an offering and give him our all.

The world would say that giving up our desires is a loss. We've been taught for years that we must put ourselves first. Our fellow man would say that we need to make ourselves a priority. But oh, are they missing out. When we give ourselves over completely to God, we get to share in his glory and in his great joy. Setting aside our earthly pleasures for heavenly treasures means we gain a lot more than what this world could ever offer us.

Empty yourself of the desires of your flesh and allow God to fill you with his presence. You won't feel a lack. In fact, God will overflow in your life, spilling out everywhere for others to see. Become less, so that you can gain more of him.

How can you make more room for Christ in your life?

God, I choose to make room for you today. This moment that I am giving to you, is a moment that I choose to fill with your Holy Spirit. Stay with me today.

In Sunshine and Storm

When times are good, be happy;
but when times are bad, consider this:
God has made the one as well as the other.
Therefore, no one can discover
anything about their future.

ECCLESIASTES 7:14 NIV

It's easy to feel happy on a sunny day, when all is well, the birds are singing, and life is going along swimmingly. But what happens when waters are rougher, bad news comes, or the days feel just plain hard?

God wants us to feel gladness when times are good. He has made each and every day. We are called to rejoice in all of them whether good or bad. Happiness is determined by our circumstances, but true joy comes when we can find the silver linings, hidden in our darkest hours—when we can sing his praises no matter what.

Is your happiness determined by your circumstance? Pray that you will discover true joy in your Creator. Ask him to give you a deep and abiding satisfaction in each day that goes beyond human understanding. We don't know what the future holds for us here on earth, but we can find our delight in the knowledge that our eternity is set in beauty.

What is the source of your happiness? Do you need to readjust what makes you truly happy?

God, you created this day. It might be raining or sunny; it might be full of troubles, or full of peace. Whatever the circumstance, help me to know your joy and your peace in everything.

A Life of Worship

I urge you, brethren, by the mercies of God, to present your bodies a living and holy sacrifice, acceptable to God, which is your spiritual service of worship.

Romans 12:1 NASB

When we are truly diving deep into a growing relationship with God, our entire lives become a living, breathing act of worship. Take your everyday moments, whether sleeping, eating, going to work, or just walking around, and give them over to God in the spirit of worship today.

The sacrifices you make, like waking up early to spend time with God instead of hitting snooze one more time, or giving up a night at home to attend an evening of prayer are examples of this kind of worship.

When you take your ordinary moments and you give them up to God, they become forms of devotion to him. Let your entire being create a beautiful song of praise to your Savior.

What are some other opportunities to worship God in your day-to-day life?

God, I am devoted to you. I don't always feel like worshiping, but I know that when I do, I bless your heart. Give me an opportunity to bless you today.

Power without Limit

Now all glory to God, who is able, through his mighty power at work within us, to accomplish infinitely more than we might ask or think. Glory to him in the church and in Christ Jesus through all generations forever and ever! Amen.

EPHESIANS 3:20-21 NLT

There is only so much that we can accomplish in our own strength. We plow through our tasks, and we can get a lot done. But we are limited in our power.

God has no limit in what he can do. If we ask him to work in our lives, there's no stopping the amazing things that will happen. We can accomplish more than we'd ever think to ask for. The best part is that he wants to do it for us.

Ask the Lord for bigger and bolder things. Pray that he will give you the supernatural ability you need to accomplish all that is before you. His power is without limits, and he will extend it to you if you'll only ask him for it! God doesn't look at your requests as a chore or another task to cross off his list so you'll stop pestering him. He loves to answer your prayer when your heart is directed toward him.

How have you experienced God's power in the past?
What do you need God's enabling power for this week?

God, I have so much to do today! I know that you can help me to organize my day so I can do more than I feel I am capable of. I know that every time I include you in my day, I seem to be more efficient. I take hold of your power at work in me.

True Riches

Whatever were gains to me I now consider loss for the sake of Christ. What is more, I consider everything a loss because of the surpassing worth of knowing Christ Jesus my Lord, for whose sake I have lost all things. I consider them garbage, that I may gain Christ and be found in him, not having a righteousness of my own that comes from the law, but that which is through faith in Christ—the righteousness that comes from God on the basis of faith. I want to know Christ—yes, to know the power of his resurrection and participation in his sufferings, becoming like him in his death, and so, somehow, attaining to the resurrection from the dead.

PHILIPPIANS 3:7-11 NIV

Once you've experienced the true beauty of a relationship with Christ, everything else becomes somehow insignificant. What you once held dear no longer seems important.

Compared to knowing Christ as your Savior, everything else the world values pales in comparison.

Have you fully embraced the ways of God? Would you be willing to lose everything for him? Grasp a hold of the beauty he is offering. Pray for a heart that's glad to be rid of earthly treasures and eager for what's in store for a true believer.

What does the resurrection mean to you?
How can you translate this meaning to an unbeliever?

God, as I get ready for a new day, I pray that I would be able to see the insignificance of some of the things that I pursue and the significance of others. I ask that you would give me discernment of what is garbage and what is treasure.

Overcome the Obstacles

"These things I have spoken to you, so that in Me you may have peace. In the world you have tribulation, but take courage; I have overcome the world."

John 16:33

Life on planet Earth is not always easy. In fact, we will go through many times of trouble. Perhaps you are in the middle of a struggle right this very moment. God has an amazing message of hope that he wants you to hear.

We have been created in his image. We are called to live a life modeled after Jesus. He tells us that he has already overcome the world. That means we are overcomers! We can take this world and all its heartaches and pain by storm. We have the biggest cheerleader standing by our side the entire time—our Lord and Savior.

When we rely on the world to bring us joy, we find only temporary happiness. But in God, we find peace. Trust him, so you have an unshakeable assurance that you can overcome the obstacles that have been placed in your path today.

What troubles are weighing you down right now?
Remember that Jesus has overcome the world.
Let this bring you peace today.

God, I know that I might face troubles today, but I trust that if I make decisions that are guided by your Holy Spirit, you will give me peace. Let my wise decisions be an example of you today.

In This Together

Christ's love compels us, because we are convinced that one died for all, and therefore all died. And he died for all, that those who live should no longer live for themselves but for him who died for them and was raised again.

2 Corinthians 5:14-15 niv

We can often find ourselves seeing all the ways we are different. You take your coffee black, and your friend takes hers with more cream than caffeine. You vote one way, your neighbor votes another. Your sister is an introvert, and your mother won't stop talking.

Here's the thing we have in common: no matter who we are or what we believe, Jesus Christ died for us all. Each and every one of us falls into the category of "all." There's nobody left out. He died for your mom, he died for your sister, and he died for your neighbor who votes differently than you do. One man died for everyone, and this puts us all on the same page.

Do you recognize your differences with others? Do you feel upset by someone's different way of doing things? Keep looking for the similarities between you and those around you. Pray that you can break down walls and stand on the truth.

What differences with others are bothering you right now?
Can you find some similarities?

God, let me put aside my differences with other people today, and instead focus on the importance that we are all equal in your sight.

Bold and Confident

My voice You shall hear in the morning, O Lord;
In the morning I will direct it to You,
And I will look up.

Psalm 5:3 NKJV

Each and every day, we are given the most incredible opportunity. We are given the chance to talk to a God who has been in our shoes—the Son of Man who literally walked the walk. He is waiting for us to walk up to him and ask him anything.

Jesus went through the same things we do during his time on earth, so he truly understands where we're coming from when we approach him. We don't need to muster up our courage! He wants us to be confident.

Esther was bold when she approached her king about saving her people, and he was known to make rash and terrible decisions. We get to talk to a King who is known for his mercy. Approach him confidently today and ask him to supply all your needs. He loves you. He understands you. He wants the best for you. He will show you grace and mercy in whatever it is that you seek.

Are you holding back tentatively in your time with your heavenly King? Be bold, and be confident!

God, I give you this space in my day. Hear my voice as I direct it to you. I look up in expectation that you hear me.

Dance Unhindered

"It was before the Lord, who chose me in place of your father and all his household, to appoint me as prince over Israel, the people of the Lord, that I have danced before the Lord. I will make myself yet more contemptible than this, and I will be abased in my own eyes; but by the maids of whom you have spoken, by them I shall be held in honor."

2 Samuel 6:21-22

Peer pressure is real even for adults. We often worry about how we will look in the eyes of others. *Do I look okay today?* we wonder. *I forgot to bring the garbage can in. What will the neighbors think?* we ask ourselves.

There was at least one person who didn't care what others thought of him. King David was so excited after winning a big battle that he went whooping and dancing, praising God as he marched home to his family. When his wife scorned him for looking foolish, he had no time for her words.

Are you worried about what others think, or are you concerned with what God thinks of you? Don't let others hold you back from expressing your faith. Choose to be real with God. Dance in his presence today no matter what you may look like! He wants to celebrate life with you.

What expression can you give God this evening for his goodness?

God, I long to be unashamed about my faith in you. I acknowledge that you bring me joy and yet often I keep it hidden because I don't want to look out of place. Grant me the spirit of King David to dance before you with all my might!

Eye on You

Because we are united with Christ, we have received an inheritance from God, for he chose us in advance, and he makes everything work out according to his plan. God's purpose was that we Jews who were the first to trust in Christ would bring praise and glory to God.

Ephesians 1:11-12 NLT

Did you know that long before you decided to take the plunge and accept Christ into your heart as your Savior, he had his eye on you? He was waiting for you to come to him so he could share with you his eternal gift. God wanted glorious living for you. And oh, how he celebrated when you made that decision!

It is through Christ that we discover who we are. When we put our hope in him, we find ourselves. It's in him that we learn what we are living for. And he works all our lives together as Christians for the greater good.

You were chosen by God. He waited for you, and he rejoiced when you came to him. Celebrate with him today. Praise him for the gift he has given you in eternal salvation. He is so good. Thank God for his plan for your life. He knows what is best for you, and he desires that you walk in the way he is leading.

How can you see God working out his plan through your life?

God, thank you that you have included me as a part of your plan. Let my life reflect your glory.

Truth about Legalism

The love of God is this, that we obey his commandments. And his commandments are not burdensome.

1 John 5:3 NRSV

When we buy into the lie that how we live our earthly lives determines whether or not we will have eternal life, we lose sight of the entire point of the Gospel. Legalism is the term for believing that doing good works will make you right with God. But the people in the Bible who dedicated their lives to doing the right thing (the Pharisees) are the very same people who put Jesus on the cross.

Legalism isn't a holier form of God-worship; it's self-worship. When we give ourselves a role in our own salvation, we are claiming to be able to do something only Jesus is capable of. The grace of Christ alone is what saves us.

Your obedience doesn't carry the weight of your righteousness. You have righteousness through faith in the Son of God. You have only to love him. In your love, you will desire to obey him because you know that obedience will bring you closer to him.

Are there things that you are doing for God
that you think will help you gain favor in his eyes?
Re-evaluate your motivations.

God, I choose this day to serve you in obedience.
I do this not because I am commanded to but because I love you.

Writing on the Wall

I will ponder the way that is blameless.
Oh when will you come to me?
I will walk with integrity of heart
within my house;
I will not set before my eyes
anything that is worthless.
I hate the work of those who fall away;
it shall not cling to me.
A perverse heart shall be far from me;
I will know nothing of evil.

Psalm 101:2-4 ESV

What types of messages do we allow to enter our homes through television, social media, internet, magazines, smartphones, or even our own conversations? Do we take the time to really ponder and evaluate the ideas that we absorb even sub-consciously?

The Holy Spirit will be your greatest ally when determining which messages you should or should not allow into your home. Listen to his prompting, and don't ignore him when he gently tells you that something isn't healthy for your spirit.

Print some of your favorite verses out and hang them on your walls. Let the messages in your home be messages of godliness. Let your loved ones see and hear the words of life and truth above those of sin and death. Choose carefully the words and images that enter your home and your heart.

In what ways have you become complacent about evil things? Remove those influences from your life.

God, thank you for giving me a good mind that can discern right and wrong. Thank you for being a living presence in me that can help me to make the right decisions. Help me to have nothing to do with evil.

He Is Good

Adam was not the one deceived; it was the woman who was deceived and became a sinner.

1 Timothy 2:14 niv

The first sin ever was committed by a woman. Eve, the mother of all, changed humanity forever when she made one fatal decision to venture outside God's boundaries. When Eve took a bite of the fruit, she did more than just give in to her own desire for pleasure, she opened the door of sin to every generation that would follow after her.

As Eve believed that God was depriving her, she also believed that God wasn't good after all—that he didn't have her best interest at heart. The moment Eve stopped believing God was good was the moment that temptation overcame her.

Eve's key mistake was that she doubted the goodness of God. The serpent knew he could penetrate a woman's mind with well-spoken words, and he convinced Eve that God was withholding something from her. How often do you doubt the goodness of God? Do you wonder if the boundaries he's put in place are really necessary or right? Do you doubt that God cares about the details of your life? Remember that God is good, and that you can trust him completely.

Are you being tempted to follow a different path?
Turn back to God and trust that he will give you the best.

God, I know that there is a temptation to doubt your goodness and to choose my own way. Teach me the truth so I don't stray from the good path you have set before me.

Our Beautiful Girlhood

His body is made new like a child's.
It will return to the way it was when he was young.
That person will pray to God, and God will listen to him.
He will see God's face and will shout with happiness.
And God will set things right for him again.

Job 33:25-26

Close your eyes for a moment and think back to when you were little. Do you see yourself? What are you like? Excitable? Passionate? Quiet? Shy? Remember for a moment what it was like to be that child: caring nothing of dirty hands or messed-up hair. Caring only for that moment—the fleeting moment of freedom and unpredictability: a child who can get lost in make-believe and dreams; one who knows how to dance wildly and run freely; a child who knows full well the arts of day dreaming and wild flower picking.

That was then, and this is now. That little kid from your childhood memory grew up quickly. Responsibility eventually overtakes carefree spontaneity. Reality drowns out limitless dreams.

Restoration of full well-being can be yours! Doesn't that sound just like childhood? How do you feel about the past? Today, forget about the things which never really mattered all that much, and remember what it is to breathe life in your lungs. Ask God to restore to you what has been lost.

Where do you need God to help you to lighten the load?
Let him release the burden on your heart
and give you freedom in your spirit.

God, restore to me the beauty of a childlike faith. I want to find favor with you simply because I delight to be called your child.

We Have Time

Be careful how you live. Don't live like fools, but like those who are wise. Make the most of every opportunity in these evil days. Don't act thoughtlessly, but understand what the Lord wants you to do.

Ephesians 5:15-17 NLT

Time is one of those things we never seem to have enough of. Many days we race against the clock to get everything done. We seem to lack the time we need for even the most important things—things like being in God's Word, spending intentional time with loved ones, or volunteering to help those in need.

At the end of the day, there is one reality we must remember: we have time for what we make time for. It's easy to feel busy, but what are we truly busying ourselves with? Are we finding time to spend browsing social media or watching re-runs of our favorite TV shows? Are we finding time to take a long shower or sleep for a few extra minutes in the morning?

Things we choose to make time for aren't always wrong, but if we feel pressed for time and are unable to spend time with the Lord, we may need to rethink where our time goes. Take a good hard look at your day today and think about how you can spend your time most wisely—in a way that will make the most of the moments and opportunities you have.

How are you spending most of your time?
Could your priorities use a re-shuffle?

God, I take this opportunity now to prioritize time with you. I pray that you would help me create more and more space for these times.

The Burning Bush

"When forty years had passed, an Angel of the Lord appeared to him in a flame of fire in a bush, in the wilderness of Mount Sinai."

Acts 7:30 NKJV

Do you ever feel like your life is in a holding pattern? Like your something big must be lurking around the next corner. You may feel like your life is being wasted while you wait for your own destiny.

God had Moses in a very similar holding pattern. He had this incredible experience at birth where he was specifically saved from certain death, miraculously found by the most powerful woman in the land, and raised as royalty. He had an unbelievable launch to his life, and then, after a fatal mistake, he became your average sheep herder in the desert for the next forty years. Forty years. That's a long time to wonder if the greatness of the vision you were born into would ever come to fruition.

The most amazing part of Moses' story is that after all the waiting, God came to him in one of the most famous ways in history—and we all know how incredibly God went on to use Moses after that. Remember, if you feel directionless right now—without vision and without destiny—know that no wilderness is too remote for you to stumble upon a burning bush. You have only to trust, to watch, and to wait.

What is God asking you to do in this moment?
Do you need to seek him or get moving?

God, even the greatest people in the Bible had their moments of failure or just waiting around. I pray that I faithfully seek your heart so that I will know when and where you want me to go. Thank you for my destiny in you.

Humility

Humility is the fear of the Lord;
its wages are riches and honor and life.

PROVERBS 22:4 NIV

God values humility over pride and earthly success. That is why sometimes God makes us wait before revealing his plans for us. In the waiting is where he grows us in humility. When things don't work out perfectly, our pride is dismantled and we learn the most valuable lessons.

In God's kingdom, humility is elevated and pride is made low. Those who are poor are rich, and those who are weak are strong. Maybe your day has not felt like a success God is more concerned with having your heart fully devoted to him than he is with you having a successful day.

God being glorified in our lives doesn't make sense to our humanity because his plan isn't our plan and his ways are different. The entire message of the Gospel is upside-down from what we know here on earth. God wants you to serve him, and he loves when you prosper in kingdom work, but those things aren't his main goal. His main goal is to be with you forever. Humble yourself in his presence today.

What kind of success are you pursuing right now?

God, thank you that my success isn't something that I have gotten to on my own. I have seen a lot of failures along the way, and I have also recognized how many people you have put in my life to help me. I acknowledge you in my success today.

True Religion

Pure and undefiled religion in the sight of our God and Father is this: to visit orphans and widows in their distress, and to keep oneself unstained by the world.

James 1:27 NASB

Many people today ask what religion can do for them. How can it alleviate their fears, save them from death, and improve their quality of life? Christianity has never been about what we can get from it.

True religion— the kind that is acceptable to God—is found in giving ourselves to those who need the most. It's not about our comfort, our happiness, or even our ticket to heaven. It's about reflecting the glory of Christ on the earth.

The tender Father heart of God is far more interested in developing your love and Christ-like character than he is in keeping you comfortable. His compassion and intense love for mankind will not be satisfied with comfortable, cushioned Christianity. If you want to bring praise to God, intentionally seek out situations where you can put into practice your undefiled religion. Make it your mission to meet needs, to love, and to bring life.

Where and when can you best respond to the needs of others around you?

God, I want to reflect your glory today. Give me the opportunity to give to those in need in any form that it might come. Give me the boldness to respond, and keep me from ignorance.

Cost of Sacrifice

The king replied to Araunah, "No, I insist on buying it, for I will not present burnt offerings to the Lord my God that have cost me nothing." So David paid him fifty pieces of silver for the threshing floor and the oxen.

2 Samuel 24:24 NLT

What are you not doing right now because of fear? Are there things you are keeping quiet about simply because you're afraid? Are there steps forward that you aren't taking because you're frightened about what may happen if you do? Are there stirrings in your heart that you're neglecting because you're afraid of how you may be criticized?

In the Bible, when God announced what he was about to do in someone's life, he often began it with the words, "Do not fear." He knew we would worry. He knew we would list the cons and stress over the details, and he said don't.

Jesus died on the cross and paid the price for our lives—not for our money or our talents. He doesn't just want the parts that others see. He wants the secret, hidden parts of us. How much are you willing to give back to God? How much are you willing to sacrifice for others? Think about this as you spend time with God.

What are you holding back from God?
In light of what his death cost him, is there really
a price too high for your sacrifice to him?

God, I know that you have great things in store for me. Help me to recognize when my fear is getting in the way. Let me put my faith into action in small ways today, so I can get used to stepping out in faith and be ready for it when you ask me to do bigger things.

Peace in Obedience

Abram believed the Lord. And the Lord accepted Abram's faith, and that faith made him right with God.

Genesis 15:6 NCV

Have you ever stepped out and said yes to something crazy for God? You followed him into the middle of the ocean and trusted him to keep you afloat. Stepping out in faith isn't easy. In fact, it's messy. It's a lot of wondering what you're doing, and why you're doing it. It's a lot of closing your eyes and begging God to remind you of all the things he placed on your heart when he originally gave you the vision.

Stepping out in faith is about boldly facing your harshest critics and telling them you're not sure if everything will work out. It's being at peace in total chaos. It's putting yourself out there and wondering if you'll live up to expectations. It's wondering if you have anything to offer after all.

There is peace in obedience—peace that even when you're criticized, laughed at, and misunderstood, the God of the universe is pleased. And everything else fades away in light of that awesome reality. If God is asking you to do something that terrifies you, step out in faith. Obey him. Believe him. It will be worth it. When you stand in the truth that you have obeyed, it doesn't really matter how everything looks or feels. What matters is that you were obedient. You believed what God was telling you.

How is God testing your faith? Are you willing to say yes?

God, I say yes to you today. Yes to your Word, yes to your calling, yes to your truth.

Storytelling

Jesus constantly used these illustrations when speaking to the crowds. In fact, because the prophets said that he would use so many, he never spoke to them without at least one illustration. For it had been prophesied, "I will talk in parables; I will explain mysteries hidden since the beginning of time."

MATTHEW 13:34-35 TLB

We enjoy listening to stories because they help us to relate with a concept and personalize an idea. We hear a lofty explanation and struggle to understand, but a story illustrates the same thought and we become connected to it.

Jesus was a storyteller. While he walked the earth, he told people many stories in order to teach them something. Jesus used parables and imagery instead of just spitting it out so that people would meditate, speculate, study, and absorb the words to better understand them. The parables that Jesus told weren't just simple stories; their symbolisms revealed secrets of the kingdom of heaven and made its glory digestible for the common man.

When people who don't know God hear the Gospel, it can be confusing because their eyes have not been opened by the Holy Spirit. When you share with them your own story of God's work in your life, their hearts and minds may be more easily opened. Take a few moments to think about who you could share your God stories with this week.

What is your story of God's work in your life?

Thank you, God, for your stories. Open my eyes to see the creativity and truth in them. Thank you that you have given me my own story. Help me to tell it in honesty and creativity, so that people's hearts and minds can be opened to the power of your grace in my life.

Appetite

"No one can serve two masters; for a slave will either hate the one and love the other, or be devoted to the one and despise the other. You cannot serve God and wealth."

MATTHEW 6:24 NRSV

Appetite is a funny thing. Our bodies have the ability to communicate hunger to our brains, and our brains then cause us to seek out a solution to the problem. When we are genuinely hungry, we look for food that will fill our stomachs and quiet our hunger.

Our souls have appetites also, but we so easily fill our time and energy with the world's entertainment. We fill ourselves up with things that will never be able to satisfy and leave little room for the only one who can.

There is a throne in your heart upon which only one master can sit—and you must choose wisely who will take residence there. Will you allow your life to be ruled by the pursuit of things which will never last, or will you accept nothing less than eternal stock for your life's investment?

Are you battling between two masters?
Ask God to help you to love him first.

God, when I get hungry today, remind me also to hunger for you. Help me to fill that hunger with goodness and not evil, so I am spiritually fit and healthy.

Continual Praise

I will bless the Lord at all times;
his praise shall continually be in my mouth.

PSALM 34:1 ESV

It's relatively easy to sing God's praises when all is going well in our lives: when he blesses us with something we asked for, when he heals us, or when he directly answers a prayer. We naturally turn and give him praise and glory for good things. What about when things aren't going well? What about in dry times, painful times, or times of waiting?

Do we only praise God for something after he's given it, or do we praise him ahead of time in faith, knowing that he will always be good no matter what happens? We should look at all difficulties in life as miracles waiting to happen—chances for God to show his goodness and bring us closer to his heart.

Choose today to have praise readily on your lips instead of complaint. Whenever you feel discontentment or frustration, replace it with praise. By focusing on the goodness of God, the hardships will lessen and your joy will increase.

What is discouraging you right now?
Praise God even in these circumstances
and let this praise lift your head and your heart.

God, this morning I choose praise. My day has barely started and I can already feel the stresses mounting, but I choose praise. Let my lips be full of joy instead of complaint.

Love that Is Felt

"These people come near to me with their mouth
and honor me with their lips,
but their hearts are far from me.
Their worship of me
is based on merely human rules they have been taught."

ISAIAH 29:13 NIV

Think about the most romantic movie you've ever seen. Two beautiful people portray an even more beautiful love on the silver screen, taking your heart on a romantic adventure as they play out passion right before your eyes. But behind the camera, do those two people really feel that love? They are actors. They are good at what they do. They can make that love story look so very real.

Is love really love when given outwardly but not felt inwardly? Even though it may look to everyone around you that you are passionately in love, if that love is not genuine in your heart, then it's not love at all. If our worship is borne out of true love and intimacy, it will go much further than the outward displays of affection. Our love will permeate our hearts and our lives. We will not just look like someone in love, we will be in love.

Do you feel like you are in love with God? Express your love to him and allow his love to overwhelm your heart in return.

When have you most felt God's love for you? How can you show him your love in return?

God, I want what I say to reflect what is coming from my heart. Help me to be honest about my worship toward you today.

A Warm Welcome

Accept one another, then, just as Christ accepted you, in order to bring praise to God.

Romans 15:7 NIV

Have you ever met someone and immediately felt a connection? Maybe you were drawn to their personality and a friendship was born. Have you ever met someone you struggled to connect with? Maybe the way they dressed, acted, talked, or chose their career was completely foreign to you.

We all have our natural friendships. We don't have to be best friends with everyone we meet because the truth of it is, we won't. But what if, despite our differences, we still accepted all those we come in contact with? As Christians, our main goal is to bring praise to God. By accepting others with the same measure of absolute acceptance that Christ extends to us, we honor God and bring him praise.

Let's strive to accept those around us and to genuinely welcome them with open arms in spite of our differences. Think of someone you need to show acceptance to and make a point of doing so this week.

Who is sitting on the outside of your circle?
Can you invite them in sometimes?

God, thank you for accepting me. Let me have the same spirit of acceptance for everyone that you do. Prompt me to lay aside personal preferences, so I can show love without bias.

Emotions

Is anyone among you suffering? Let him pray.
Is anyone cheerful? Let him sing praise.

James 5:13 esv

It is no secret that women can be emotional. They are complicated creatures who feel deeply. Sometimes their emotions make them feel like a bit of a mess, so they try to hide them from those nearby—and even from God.

God created us to live with a full range of emotions. He is aware how those feelings directly impact our daily lives. God is not frustrated with us as we feel all the things that he created us to feel. He is not offended by our anger, impatient with our tears, or bothered by our laughter.

Don't be tempted to come to God with your emotions covered up. Allow him to see your raw emotion in all its honesty. Lay everything before him, holding nothing back. He loves you and he will stick with you through good times and bad. In the same way, approach others with an openness to their emotions. Pray when they are suffering and sing praise when they are cheerful.

What are you feeling right now? What have your emotions been like lately? Embrace the gift of sharing your emotions.

God, I will probably feel a range of emotions today. Let me recognize this as what you have created as part of my humanity and let me accept emotions for what they are.

No Condemnation

Straightening up, Jesus said to her, "Woman, where are they? Did no one condemn you?" She said, "No one, Lord." And Jesus said, "I do not condemn you either. Go. From now on sin no more."

John 8:10-11 NASB

Most of us know the story of the woman caught in adultery. One of the intriguing moments was when Jesus was questioned about whether or not the woman should be stoned. His response is to stoop down and start writing in the dirt. Jesus' action of stooping in the dirt literally defines one interpretation of the word *grace*.

As others stood casting judgement, Jesus removed himself from the accusers, stooping low and occupying himself elsewhere. It spoke volumes about his lack of participation in the crowd's judgement. Because of Jesus' distraction, the eyes of the onlookers were drawn off the woman, perhaps lifting a portion of her shame. With their attention focused on Jesus, he said the words that saved the woman's life: "Let him who has never sinned cast the first stone." One by one, the accusers walked away.

Jesus was the only one qualified to stone the adulterous woman. This is a beautiful foreshadowing of the redemption he later brought to all sinners. Beloved, Jesus is the only one qualified to condemn you, and he chose to condemn himself instead. You are free and clean because of the grace of Jesus Christ.

What do you need forgiveness for? Bring it to Jesus who is full of compassion for you.

God, this picture of your grace brings me to tears. I am humbled by your graciousness toward someone who was being accused so harshly. Thank you that you show the same grace toward me. Forgive me in this moment and wash me with your love.

Perseverance

Do not throw away this confident trust in the Lord. Remember the great reward it brings you! Patient endurance is what you need now, so that you will continue to do God's will. Then you will receive all that he has promised.

Hebrews 10:35-36 NLT

Do you remember when you first decided to follow Christ? Maybe you felt like a huge weight was being lifted off you, or that the peace and joy you'd been searching for was finally yours. You were filled with excitement in your newfound life, and you felt ready to take on the world in the name of Jesus.

Following God may come easy at first. We accept him into our lives and are swept into his love with incredible hope. But as time goes on, old temptations return, and threaten to shake our resolve. The confidence we felt in our relationship at first lessens as we wonder if we have what it takes to stick it out in this Christian life.

Perhaps you have lost the confidence you had at first. Or maybe you are still in that place of complete confidence and trust. Either way, step boldly forward into all that God has for you. Remain confident in him; he will accomplish what he has promised. When following God gets hard, press in even harder and remember that you will be richly rewarded for your perseverance.

What are you waiting on God for? Pray for patient endurance, and wait in hope and expectation.

God, sometimes I doubt who you are and what you have done. I know that you don't mind that kind of honesty. Please come alongside me in times of doubt so that even if I don't understand this faith, I can be assured of your nearness to me. Let me live another day for you today.

Perfect Love

We know the love that God has for us, and we trust that love. God is love. Those who live in love live in God, and God lives in them. This is how love is made perfect in us: that we can be without fear on the day God judges us, because in this world we are like him.

1 John 4:16-17 NCV

Does anyone know the real you? The you that hasn't been edited or exaggerated? Putting up a false front in our relationships is a direct expression of our own fear.

When we are afraid to be truly known, we lose out on the most incredible gift that can be given in relationship—honest love. We sacrifice genuine relationship on the altar of our own insecurity and fear. Try to be real with others you come in contact with today.

It's a wonderful cycle that is hard to break. You love God, he lives in you, you love him more, he lives in you more. We love because he is in us, and he is in us because we love him. It's amazing and wonderful, and you can rest assured that you are not judged for what you have done, you are judged for the love of God that is in you. You can't escape him!

Are you afraid to be fully known? Lay down your need to be perceived as perfect, and allow yourself to be loved for who you truly are. Let your fear be washed away by the perfect love of a perfect God.

God, you are love. That truth needs to sink into my heart this morning. I want to trust your love more than I have before, so much that it lives in me and overflows out of my life into the lives of those around me.

"Let them make Me a sanctuary,
that I may dwell among them."

Exodus 25:8 NKJV

Since sin entered the world in the Garden of Eden there has been a divide between the holy God and humanity. But throughout history, God has created ways for us to still have fellowship with him despite our inability to save ourselves.

God created temples and priests in the Old Testament, and then Jesus lived, died, and was resurrected to change the old system. It is no longer in places but in our hearts that God dwells.

God wants to be with us. He didn't shrug his shoulders when sin entered the world and resign himself to the fact that he wouldn't be able to have a close relationship with us any longer. Rather, God went to the greatest lengths to still be with us because his love for us is that intense. He wants to dwell among us. Not just visit. Not just talk sometimes. He wants his presence to be constantly among us.

Are you creating a sanctuary in your life where God can dwell? Are you fostering an atmosphere that will welcome the holy God? He longs to be near you.

God, dwell in my heart today. I am not worthy, but I know that through your Son, Jesus, I have been made worthy.

Money Trouble

Keep your lives free from the love of money,
and be content with what you have; for he has said,
"I will never leave you or forsake you."

HEBREWS 13:5 NRSV

Sometimes money is like water in our hands. It slips right through our fingers, and is gone as soon as it is acquired. Right after God tells us not to love money, he reminds us that he'll never leave or forsake us. He knew that we would worry about our finances. He knew that fear would come far more easily than contentment.

As Christians, we know that we should trust God with our every need. But do we really? Are we confident that no matter what circumstances come our way, God is going to take care of our finances? Or do we become consumed with worry that we will not have enough?

Remember that no matter how little or how much money you have, God is control. He is more than able to provide for all your needs and he will never forsake you.

What are you spending money on right now?
Are you content with what you have?

God, I invite you into my financial life today. I know that you are involved in all parts of life and that you know the wisest way about everything. Please guide me in wisdom with money; let me not fall into the trap of spending more than I need to.

The Right Rest

"My Presence will go with you, and I will give you rest."

Exodus 33:14 NIV

Women tend to be expert multitaskers. They juggle many responsibilities, schedules, and details. As the holiday season approaches, these tasks only seem to increase. Between the cooking and decorating, the parties and festivities—they can easily get tired out.

God says in his Word, "Be still and know that I am God." He asks us to stop, to sit, and rest because he designed us to need rest. There is a reason God set the example by resting on the seventh day after he made the world. Even the Creator knew the importance of rest.

Have you ever gotten up from the couch and still felt weary—sometimes even wearier than when you sat down? Don't confuse resting your body with resting your soul. True life-giving rest comes only from being in the presence of the Father. Pause within the busyness of the impending holiday season to sit before God, read his Word, and wait on him as you recharge in his presence.

Where have you most sensed the Lord's presence today?

God, in the stillness of the moment, fill my heart with peace that will last me for the day ahead.

Pure Water

I want more than anything
to be in the courtyards of the Lord's Temple.
My whole being wants
to be with the living God.

Psalm 84:2 NCV

Have you ever noticed that the more consistently you drink water, the more your body thirsts for it? And the less you drink water, the less you consciously desire it. Though you still need water to live, you become satisfied with small amounts of it disguised in other foods and drinks. But for a body that has become accustomed to pure water on a daily basis, only straight water will quench its thirst.

The same principle applies to God's presence in our lives. The more we enter his presence, the more we long to stay there. The more we sit at his feet and listen to what he has to say, the more we need his Word to continue living. If we allow ourselves to become satisfied with candy-coated truth and second-hand revelation, we will slowly begin to lose our hunger for the pure, untainted presence of the living God.

Does your entire being long to be with God? Press into Jesus until you can no longer be satisfied with anything less than the purest form of his presence. Cultivate your hunger and your fascination with him until you literally crave him. Spend your life feasting on his truth, knowing his character, and adoring his heart.

What does it look like for you to be in the courtyards of the Lord's temple? Spend some time there today.

God, let my thirst for you return. I can never get enough of your presence, but often I don't find myself feeling like I need you and that's because I haven't been seeking you. I pray as I start the day that you would fill me so I will continue to desire you more.

Prepared to Serve

"Very truly, I tell you, the Son can do nothing on his own, but only what he sees the Father doing; for whatever the Father does, the Son does likewise. The Father loves the Son and shows him all that he himself is doing; and he will show him greater works than these, so that you will be astonished."

John 5:19-20 NRSV

A natural response to feeling the love of God is to want to do things for him. But we have to become people of God before we can effectively do God's work. The only way to become his people is to spend time in his presence.

The disciples didn't go directly from responding to God's call to full time, full blown ministry. They spent a lot of time with Jesus first—learning from him, talking with him, and watching him minister. Not even Jesus acted without first paying attention to what God was saying.

Take time to be quiet before God and ponder his words and his plans. Through knowing his heart, you will discover where he is already working and you will be able to join him in his will.

What is the Father doing in your life,
or in the things around you, right now?
Take your cue from what he is doing.

Jesus, I want to learn more about you so I can imitate you. Lead me to great books about you, lead me to great teaching about you, and most importantly lead me to your living Word, where I can know you the best.

Giving Thanks

Swing wide, you gates of righteousness,
and let me pass through,
and I will enter into your presence to worship only you!
I have found the gateway to God,
the pathway to his presence for all his lovers.

Psalm 118:19-20 TPT

What happens in our souls when we say thank you to God? When we consecrate a passing second by breathing gratitude into it? What happens to our very being when we acknowledge the weight and glory of even the most insignificant gift?

With each moment of paused reflection, each thank-filled statement, we are set free. Set free from negativity. Set free from dark thoughts of death, pain, suffering, and ugliness. We enter his gates with thanksgiving. We enter his holy place. We walk directly through the door he created.

To walk in thanksgiving is to walk right into God's presence. This season of thanksgiving has a way of taking our hearts and righting them. It opens our eyes to wonder and splendor in casual moments. It puts things into perspective and restores triumph to the defeated soul. Practice saying thank you today—knowing that through your thankfulness, you will usher yourself into the presence of God.

What are you thankful for today?
How has God brought these things into your life?

Father, thank you for all that you have done in this earth, in my family, and in my life. I am grateful for you bringing me through difficult times and joyful times. I choose to thank you in the middle of this crazy life, because I owe it all to you.

Rejoice, Pray, Thank

*Rejoice always, pray without ceasing,
give thanks in all circumstances; for this is
the will of God in Christ Jesus for you.*

1 THESSALONIANS 5:16-18 NRSV

It is easy for us to get weighed down with the negative things in this world. Our lives, and the lives of those around us, are full of troubles that make us weary. Some days it can be difficult to find joy in the middle of our own chaos.

We wonder what God's will is especially in the hardships. We can't see his master plan, but feel as though if we could, maybe we could make it through. We wonder what God wants us to do through our difficulties.

These three things: constant rejoicing, prayer, and thanksgiving are the formula for successfully doing God's will in our lives. Take this moment to think about what you're thankful for. Rejoice continually in what God has done for you. Thank God intentionally for those things.

Who would be thinking about you right now and being thankful for you in their lives? Acknowledge that you are a blessing to others too!

God, I have a big list of things to be thankful for. I choose to dwell on these things because they bring me joy and it reminds me of what a blessed life you have given me. You know that things have been difficult and there are times when I have doubted your goodness, and yet, in this moment, I see your care for me in so many ways. Thank you.

Perfect

His divine power has granted to us everything pertaining to life and godliness, through the true knowledge of Him who called us by His own glory and excellence.

2 Peter 1:3 nasb

Each of us is keenly aware of our own weaknesses. We know all our flaws too well and we make eliminating them our goal. But no matter how much effort we put out, we can never, and will never, achieve perfection.

Despite most of us realizing that we will never be perfect, we still put unreasonable pressure on ourselves. Whether in a task, in our character, or in our walk with Christ, we easily become frustrated when we reach for perfection and can't grasp it. If we allow perfectionism to drive our performance, then we will quench our own potential and inhibit our effectiveness.

God gives you the freedom to not be perfect. In fact, his power is all the more perfect when displayed in your weakness because when you aren't the main point, Jesus is. When you mess up, God has to take over and the result of that action is always perfection. Think about what it means to be made perfect through Jesus. Can you truly accept your perfection in light of what he has done for you?

Where can you see God's perfection shining through your imperfection?

God, thank you that this life is not about my perfection, but about yours. I will do my best to imitate your glory and excellence, but I know that this only comes by your grace. Help me to experience this today.

Stillness

"Be still, and know that I am God;
I will be exalted among the nations,
I will be exalted in the earth!"

Psalm 46:10 NKJV

Dusk settles on a chilly winter night. A gray fog hovers and snow begins to fall: cold, blustering snow…the kind that sticks. The snow keeps coming until you can barely see one hundred feet in front of you. In the woods, it's quiet; all you can hear is the gentle wind, and all you can see is snow and trees. A pure white blanket of snow restores the earth, and as it falls, it restores you.

Sometimes we have to get outside of the noise and chaos of our own four walls. We have to step out into the snow, or the sun, or the breeze. We have to get alone, get silent, and clear the clutter from our minds and hearts as we stand in God's natural sanctuary.

There is so much power in the stillness of knowing God as you stand serene in the world he created. The busyness of your life will always be there, but never forget to take the moments you can, to stop and know your God. In those moments, you will find refreshment and strength to take on whatever will come next.

What thoughts come to you while you are waiting in the stillness? Can you see, feel, or hear God in the quiet?

God, it is so right to have this time to be still. Thank you for the quietness and stillness of today. Sometimes I dread it. Let me rest in the peace and quiet and hand my thoughts and hopes over to you.

It's a Wonderful Life

The mind of man plans his way,
But the Lord directs his steps.

PROVERBS 16:9 NASB

Have you ever seen the holiday movie "It's a Wonderful Life"? It's an old classic, and it's easy to see why when you watch it. The feelings of the actors onscreen are so pure and raw—and utterly relatable. We have a lot of nights similar to those in the movie: nights where everything goes wrong and we ask, "Why?"

There are many things in our lives that we simply don't get. We aren't sure why some things happen and other things don't. We have our own lofty dreams and treasured plans, and when they don't work out the way they did in our hearts or minds, we feel lost, angry, and confused.

When everything goes wrong and the plans in our hearts don't work out, God knows what he's doing. He sees what we do not. We can have the best ideas in the world, but if God is not directing us, our plans will falter. Trust in God with all of your heart. Dedicate your plans to him, and allow him to make you his perfect masterpiece.

What are some of your plans for the future?
Commit them to God, asking him to direct your steps.

Father, this verse is a great reminder when I am questioning why things around me are going the way they are. I want to control what happens, and yet I can't. Give me the grace to let go and let you direct my steps.